W9-AZK-087

THIS JOURNAL
BELONGS TO
AN AWESOME
KID CALLED

Boone

Copyright © 2019

HOW TO USE THIS GRATITUDE JOURNAL

SIMPLY COMPLETE ONE PAGE A DAY WITH ANSWERS THAT INSPIRE YOU AND SPARK GRATITUDE. REMEMBER TO COMPLETE THE LAST QUESTION AT THE END OF THE DAY

M T (W) TH F S SU   DATE: 12 / 10 / 20

I THANK THE LORD FOR

1. My family, for always loving me
2. Hearing my prayers every morning
3. My good health and clever brain!

TODAY I WILL STRIVE TO BE:

More patient when my baby sister cries at night

BIBLE VERSE OF THE DAY | *The Lord your God is with you*

(JOSHUA 1:9)

BLESSINGS THE DAY BROUGHT ME

My family came to see me
perform with the church choir!
I was really nervous at first
but s

DOODLE OF THE DAY!

M T W TH F S SU   DATE: 10 / 21 / 2022

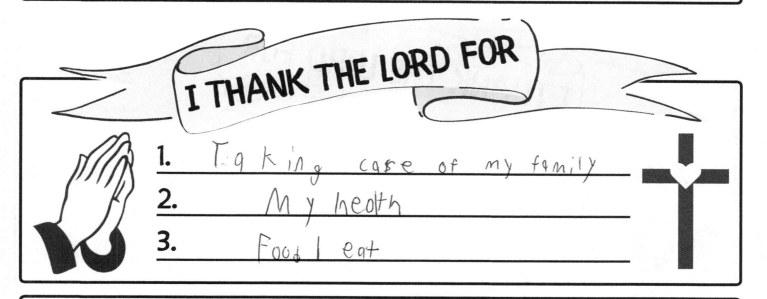

I THANK THE LORD FOR

1. Taking care of my family
2. My health
3. Food I eat

TODAY I WILL STRIVE TO BE:

A good boy

BIBLE VERSE OF THE DAY

I delight to do Your will, my God;
Your instruction lives within me

(PSALM 40:8)

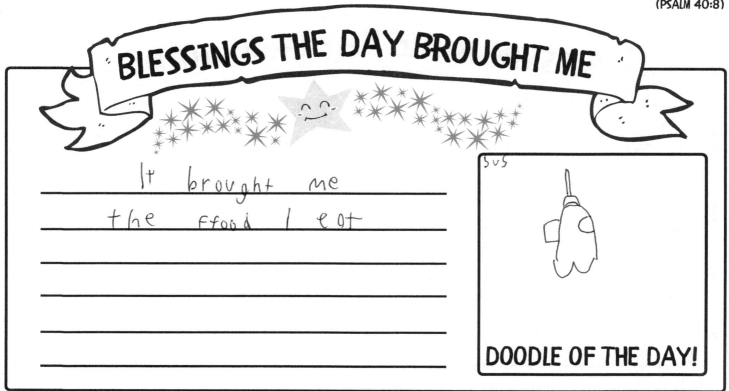

BLESSINGS THE DAY BROUGHT ME

It brought me the food I eat

sus

DOODLE OF THE DAY!

M	T	W	TH	F	S	SU	DATE: _1_ / _11_ / _23_

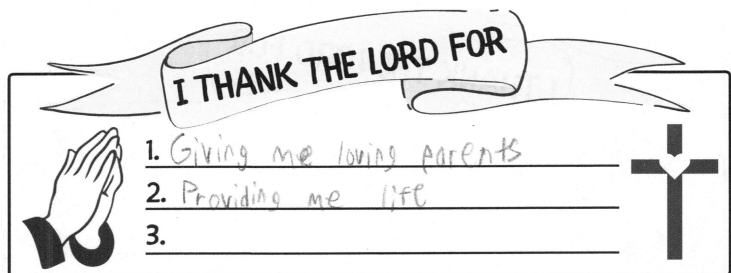

I THANK THE LORD FOR

1. Giving me loving parents
2. Providing me life
3. _____

TODAY I WILL STRIVE TO BE:

More obedient

BIBLE VERSE OF THE DAY	*God created man in His own image*

(GENESIS 1:27A)

BLESSINGS THE DAY BROUGHT ME

_____
_____
_____
_____
_____

DOODLE OF THE DAY!

| M T W TH F S SU | DATE: _1_ / _14_ / _25_ |

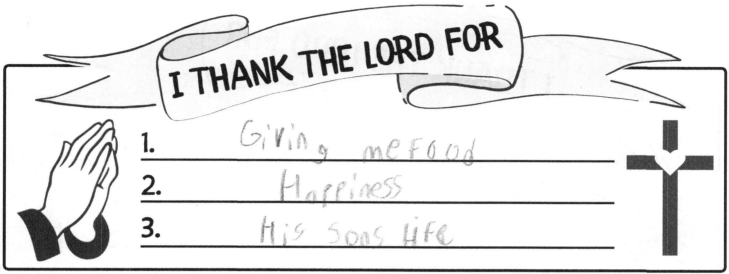

I THANK THE LORD FOR

1. Giving me food
2. Happiness
3. His sons life

TODAY I WILL STRIVE TO BE:

Helpful

| **BIBLE VERSE OF THE DAY** | *Honor your father and your mother* |

(EXODUS 20:12A)

BLESSINGS THE DAY BROUGHT ME

_____

_____

_____

_____

_____

DOODLE OF THE DAY!

M   T   W   TH   F   S   SU   DATE: ___ / ___ / ___

I THANK THE LORD FOR

1. _____
2. _____
3. _____

TODAY I WILL STRIVE TO BE:

_____

BIBLE VERSE OF THE DAY | *Love the Lord your God with all your heart, with all your soul, and with all your strength*

(DEUTERONOMY 6:5)

BLESSINGS THE DAY BROUGHT ME

_____
_____
_____
_____
_____

DOODLE OF THE DAY!

M T W TH F S SU   DATE: ___/___/___

I THANK THE LORD FOR

1. _____
2. _____
3. _____

TODAY I WILL STRIVE TO BE:

_____

BIBLE VERSE OF THE DAY | *For the Lord watches over the way of the righteous*

(PSALM 1:6A)

BLESSINGS THE DAY BROUGHT ME

_____
_____
_____
_____
_____

DOODLE OF THE DAY!

M   T   W   TH   F   S   SU   DATE: ___/___/___

I THANK THE LORD FOR

1. _____

2. _____

3. _____

TODAY I WILL STRIVE TO BE:

_____

BIBLE VERSE OF THE DAY | *You are to keep My commands and do them*

(LEVITICUS 22:31)

BLESSINGS THE DAY BROUGHT ME

_____

_____

_____

_____

_____

DOODLE OF THE DAY!

| M T W TH F S SU | DATE: ___ / ___ / ___ |

I THANK THE LORD FOR

1. _____
2. _____
3. _____

TODAY I WILL STRIVE TO BE:

_____

BIBLE VERSE OF THE DAY

This is the day the Lord has made; let us rejoice and be glad in it

(PSALM 118:24)

BLESSINGS THE DAY BROUGHT ME

_____
_____
_____
_____
_____

DOODLE OF THE DAY!

| M T W TH F S SU | DATE: ___/___/___ |

I THANK THE LORD FOR

1. _____
2. _____
3. _____

TODAY I WILL STRIVE TO BE:

_____

BIBLE VERSE OF THE DAY | *Give thanks to the Lord, for He is good. His love is eternal*

(PSALM 136:1)

BLESSINGS THE DAY BROUGHT ME

_____
_____
_____
_____
_____

DOODLE OF THE DAY!

M   T   W   TH   F   S   SU   DATE: ___ / ___ / ___

I THANK THE LORD FOR

1. _____
2. _____
3. _____

TODAY I WILL STRIVE TO BE:

_____

BIBLE VERSE OF THE DAY

I will praise You because I have been remarkably and wonderfully made

(PSALM 139:14)

BLESSINGS THE DAY BROUGHT ME

_____
_____
_____
_____
_____

DOODLE OF THE DAY!

M T W TH F S SU   DATE: ___ / ___ / ___

I THANK THE LORD FOR

1. _____

2. _____

3. _____

TODAY I WILL STRIVE TO BE:

_____

BIBLE VERSE OF THE DAY | *Search me, God, and know my heart; test me and know my concerns*

(PSALM 139:23)

BLESSINGS THE DAY BROUGHT ME

_____

_____

_____

_____

_____

_____

DOODLE OF THE DAY!

M T W TH F S SU   DATE: __ / __ / __

I THANK THE LORD FOR

1. _____
2. _____
3. _____

TODAY I WILL STRIVE TO BE:

_____

BIBLE VERSE OF THE DAY

For the Lord gives wisdom; from His mouth come knowledge and understanding

(PROVERBS 2:6)

BLESSINGS THE DAY BROUGHT ME

_____
_____
_____
_____
_____

DOODLE OF THE DAY!

M T W TH F S SU   DATE: ___ / ___ / ___

I THANK THE LORD FOR

1. _____
2. _____
3. _____

TODAY I WILL STRIVE TO BE:

_____

BIBLE VERSE OF THE DAY | The rich and the poor have this in common: the Lord made them both

(PROVERBS 22:2)

BLESSINGS THE DAY BROUGHT ME

_____
_____
_____
_____
_____

DOODLE OF THE DAY!

M T W TH F S SU   DATE: ___/___/___

I THANK THE LORD FOR

1. _____
2. _____
3. _____

TODAY I WILL STRIVE TO BE:

_____

BIBLE VERSE OF THE DAY | *Every word of God is pure; He is a shield to those who take refuge in Him*

(PROVERBS 30:5)

BLESSINGS THE DAY BROUGHT ME

_____
_____
_____
_____
_____

DOODLE OF THE DAY!

M   T   W   TH   F   S   SU   DATE: ___ / ___ / ___

I THANK THE LORD FOR

1. _____
2. _____
3. _____

TODAY I WILL STRIVE TO BE:

_____

BIBLE VERSE OF THE DAY | *Come to Me, all of you who are weary and burdened, and I will give you rest*

(MATTHEW 11:28)

BLESSINGS THE DAY BROUGHT ME

_____
_____
_____
_____
_____

DOODLE OF THE DAY!

M T W TH F S SU   DATE: ___ / ___ / ___

I THANK THE LORD FOR

1. _____
2. _____
3. _____

TODAY I WILL STRIVE TO BE:

_____

BIBLE VERSE OF THE DAY | *Just as you want others to do for you, do the same for them*

(LUKE 6:31)

BLESSINGS THE DAY BROUGHT ME

_____
_____
_____
_____
_____

DOODLE OF THE DAY!

M   T   W   TH   F   S   SU   DATE: ___ / ___ / ___

I THANK THE LORD FOR

1. _____
2. _____
3. _____

TODAY I WILL STRIVE TO BE:

_____

BIBLE VERSE OF THE DAY | *In the beginning was the Word, and the Word was with God, and the Word was God*

(JOHN 1:1)

BLESSINGS THE DAY BROUGHT ME

_____
_____
_____
_____
_____

DOODLE OF THE DAY!

M   T   W   TH   F   S   SU   DATE: __ / __ / __

I THANK THE LORD FOR

1. _____
2. _____
3. _____

TODAY I WILL STRIVE TO BE:

_____

BIBLE VERSE OF THE DAY | *For everyone who calls on the name of the Lord will be saved*

(ROMANS 10:13)

BLESSINGS THE DAY BROUGHT ME

_____
_____
_____
_____
_____

DOODLE OF THE DAY!

M T W TH F S SU   DATE: ___/___/___

I THANK THE LORD FOR

1. _____
2. _____
3. _____

TODAY I WILL STRIVE TO BE:

_____

BIBLE VERSE OF THE DAY | *Do not be conquered by evil, but conquer evil with good*

(ROMANS 12:21)

BLESSINGS THE DAY BROUGHT ME

_____
_____
_____
_____
_____

DOODLE OF THE DAY!

M T W TH F S SU   DATE: ___ / ___ / ___

I THANK THE LORD FOR

1. _____
2. _____
3. _____

TODAY I WILL STRIVE TO BE:

_____

| BIBLE VERSE OF THE DAY | I will be a Father to you, and you will be sons and daughters to Me, says the Lord |

(2 CORINTHIANS 6:18)

BLESSINGS THE DAY BROUGHT ME

_____
_____
_____
_____
_____

DOODLE OF THE DAY!

M T W TH F S SU DATE: ___ / ___ / ___

I THANK THE LORD FOR

1. _____
2. _____
3. _____

TODAY I WILL STRIVE TO BE:

_____

BIBLE VERSE OF THE DAY | *Serve one another through love*

(GALATIANS 5:13C)

BLESSINGS THE DAY BROUGHT ME

_____
_____
_____
_____
_____

DOODLE OF THE DAY!

M T W TH F S SU   DATE: __/__/__

I THANK THE LORD FOR

1. _____
2. _____
3. _____

TODAY I WILL STRIVE TO BE:

_____

BIBLE VERSE OF THE DAY | *We must not get tired of doing good, for we will reap at the proper time*

(GALATIANS 6:9)

BLESSINGS THE DAY BROUGHT ME

_____
_____
_____
_____
_____

DOODLE OF THE DAY!

M T W TH F S SU   DATE: ___ / ___ / ___

I THANK THE LORD FOR

1. _____
2. _____
3. _____

TODAY I WILL STRIVE TO BE:

_____

BIBLE VERSE OF THE DAY | *And be kind and compassionate to one another, forgiving one another*

(EPHESIANS 4:32)

BLESSINGS THE DAY BROUGHT ME

_____
_____
_____
_____
_____

DOODLE OF THE DAY!

| M | T | W | TH | F | S | SU | DATE: __ / __ / __ |

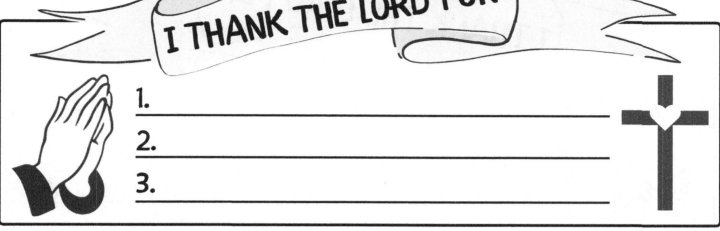

I THANK THE LORD FOR

1. _____
2. _____
3. _____

TODAY I WILL STRIVE TO BE:

_____

BIBLE VERSE OF THE DAY | *I am able to do all things through Him who strengthens me*

(PHILIPPIANS 4:13)

BLESSINGS THE DAY BROUGHT ME

_____
_____
_____
_____
_____

DOODLE OF THE DAY!

M T W TH F S SU   DATE: __/__/__

I THANK THE LORD FOR

1. _____
2. _____
3. _____

TODAY I WILL STRIVE TO BE:

_____

BIBLE VERSE OF THE DAY

Children, obey your parents in everything, for this pleases the Lord

(COLOSSIANS 3:20)

BLESSINGS THE DAY BROUGHT ME

_____
_____
_____
_____
_____

DOODLE OF THE DAY!

M T W TH F S SU   DATE: ___ / ___ / ___

I THANK THE LORD FOR

1. _____
2. _____
3. _____

TODAY I WILL STRIVE TO BE:

_____

BIBLE VERSE OF THE DAY | *Jesus Christ is the same yesterday, today, and forever*

(HEBREWS 13:8)

BLESSINGS THE DAY BROUGHT ME

_____
_____
_____
_____

DOODLE OF THE DAY!

| M T W TH F S SU | DATE: ___ / ___ / ___ |

I THANK THE LORD FOR

1. _____

2. _____

3. _____

TODAY I WILL STRIVE TO BE:

_____

BIBLE VERSE OF THE DAY

The one who does not love does not know God, because God is love

(1 JOHN 4:8)

BLESSINGS THE DAY BROUGHT ME

_____

_____

_____

_____

_____

DOODLE OF THE DAY!

M   T   W   TH   F   S   SU   DATE: ___/___/___

I THANK THE LORD FOR

1. _____
2. _____
3. _____

TODAY I WILL STRIVE TO BE:

_____

| BIBLE VERSE OF THE DAY | Rejoice in the Lord always. I will say it again: Rejoice! |

(PHILIPPIANS 4:4)

BLESSINGS THE DAY BROUGHT ME

_____
_____
_____
_____
_____

DOODLE OF THE DAY!

| M | T | W | TH | F | S | SU | DATE: ___ / ___ / ___ |

I THANK THE LORD FOR

1. _____
2. _____
3. _____

TODAY I WILL STRIVE TO BE:

_____

BIBLE VERSE OF THE DAY | *God loves a cheerful giver*

(2 CORINTHIANS 9:7C)

BLESSINGS THE DAY BROUGHT ME

_____
_____
_____
_____
_____

DOODLE OF THE DAY!

M T W TH F S SU   DATE: __ / __ / __

I THANK THE LORD FOR

1. _____
2. _____
3. _____

TODAY I WILL STRIVE TO BE:

_____

BIBLE VERSE OF THE DAY | *God is not mocked. For whatever a man sows he will also reap*

(GALATIANS 6:7)

BLESSINGS THE DAY BROUGHT ME

_____
_____
_____
_____
_____

DOODLE OF THE DAY!

M T W TH F S SU   DATE: ___/___/___

I THANK THE LORD FOR

1. _____
2. _____
3. _____

TODAY I WILL STRIVE TO BE:

_____

BIBLE VERSE OF THE DAY | Since you put away lying, Speak the truth, each one to his neighbor

(EPHESIANS 4:25)

BLESSINGS THE DAY BROUGHT ME

_____
_____
_____
_____
_____

DOODLE OF THE DAY!

M T W TH F S SU   DATE: __ / __ / __

I THANK THE LORD FOR

1. _____
2. _____
3. _____

TODAY I WILL STRIVE TO BE:

_____

BIBLE VERSE OF THE DAY | *Set your minds on what is above, not on what is on the earth*

(COLOSSIANS 3:2)

BLESSINGS THE DAY BROUGHT ME

_____
_____
_____
_____
_____

DOODLE OF THE DAY!

| M | T | W | TH | F | S | SU | DATE: ___ / ___ / ___ |

I THANK THE LORD FOR

1. _____
2. _____
3. _____

TODAY I WILL STRIVE TO BE:

_____

BIBLE VERSE OF THE DAY | So they said, "Believe in the Lord Jesus, and you will be saved"

(ACTS 16:31)

BLESSINGS THE DAY BROUGHT ME

_____
_____
_____
_____
_____
_____

DOODLE OF THE DAY!

M T W TH F S SU   DATE: ___/___/___

I THANK THE LORD FOR

1. _____
2. _____
3. _____

TODAY I WILL STRIVE TO BE:

_____

BIBLE VERSE OF THE DAY | *For Christ is the end of the law for righteousness to everyone who believes*

(ROMANS 10:4)

BLESSINGS THE DAY BROUGHT ME

_____
_____
_____
_____
_____

DOODLE OF THE DAY!

M   T   W   TH   F   S   SU   DATE: ___ / ___ / ___

I THANK THE LORD FOR

1. _____
2. _____
3. _____

TODAY I WILL STRIVE TO BE:

_____

BIBLE VERSE OF THE DAY | "I am the good shepherd. The good shepherd lays down his life for the sheep"

(JOHN 10:11)

BLESSINGS THE DAY BROUGHT ME

_____
_____
_____
_____
_____

DOODLE OF THE DAY!

M T W TH F S SU   DATE: ___ / ___ / ___

I THANK THE LORD FOR

1. _____
2. _____
3. _____

TODAY I WILL STRIVE TO BE:

_____

BIBLE VERSE OF THE DAY

For where your treasure is, there your heart will be also

(LUKE 12:34)

BLESSINGS THE DAY BROUGHT ME

_____
_____
_____
_____
_____

DOODLE OF THE DAY!

M   T   W   TH   F   S   SU   DATE: ___/___/___

I THANK THE LORD FOR

1. _____
2. _____
3. _____

TODAY I WILL STRIVE TO BE:

_____

BIBLE VERSE OF THE DAY | *For God so loved the world that He gave His one and only Son*

(JOHN 3:16A)

BLESSINGS THE DAY BROUGHT ME

_____
_____
_____
_____
_____

DOODLE OF THE DAY!

M T W TH F S SU   DATE: ___/___/___

I THANK THE LORD FOR

1. _____
2. _____
3. _____

TODAY I WILL STRIVE TO BE:

_____

BIBLE VERSE OF THE DAY | *We must obey God rather than men*

(ACTS 5:29B)

BLESSINGS THE DAY BROUGHT ME

_____
_____
_____
_____
_____

DOODLE OF THE DAY!

M T W TH F S SU   DATE: ___/___/___

I THANK THE LORD FOR

1. _____
2. _____
3. _____

TODAY I WILL STRIVE TO BE:

_____

BIBLE VERSE OF THE DAY | *Love does no wrong to a neighbor. Love, therefore, is the fulfillment of the law*

(ROMANS 13:10)

BLESSINGS THE DAY BROUGHT ME

_____
_____
_____
_____
_____

DOODLE OF THE DAY!

M T W TH F S SU   DATE: ___ /___ /___

I THANK THE LORD FOR

1. _____
2. _____
3. _____

TODAY I WILL STRIVE TO BE:

_____

| BIBLE VERSE OF THE DAY | Jesus is the Messiah, the Son of God |

(JOHN 20:31B)

BLESSINGS THE DAY BROUGHT ME

_____
_____
_____
_____
_____

DOODLE OF THE DAY!

M T W TH F S SU   DATE: ___/___/___

I THANK THE LORD FOR

1. _____
2. _____
3. _____

TODAY I WILL STRIVE TO BE:

_____

BIBLE VERSE OF THE DAY | *Jesus healed many people*

(LUKE 7:21B)

BLESSINGS THE DAY BROUGHT ME

_____
_____
_____
_____
_____

DOODLE OF THE DAY!

M T W TH F S SU   DATE: __ /__ /__

I THANK THE LORD FOR

1. _____
2. _____
3. _____

TODAY I WILL STRIVE TO BE:

_____

BIBLE VERSE OF THE DAY | *When you host a banquet, invite those who are poor, maimed, lame, or blind*

(LUKE 14:13)

BLESSINGS THE DAY BROUGHT ME

_____
_____
_____
_____

DOODLE OF THE DAY!

M T W TH F S SU   DATE: ___ / ___ / ___

I THANK THE LORD FOR

1. _____
2. _____
3. _____

TODAY I WILL STRIVE TO BE:

_____

BIBLE VERSE OF THE DAY

Have courage! It is I. Don't be afraid

(MARK 6:50)

BLESSINGS THE DAY BROUGHT ME

_____
_____
_____
_____
_____
_____

DOODLE OF THE DAY!

M T W TH F S SU   DATE: ___/___/___

I THANK THE LORD FOR

1. _____
2. _____
3. _____

TODAY I WILL STRIVE TO BE:

_____

BIBLE VERSE OF THE DAY | *Heaven and earth will pass away, but My words will never pass away*

(MARK 13:31)

BLESSINGS THE DAY BROUGHT ME

_____
_____
_____
_____
_____

DOODLE OF THE DAY!

| M T W TH F S SU | DATE: __ / __ / __ |

I THANK THE LORD FOR

1. _____
2. _____
3. _____

TODAY I WILL STRIVE TO BE:

_____

BIBLE VERSE OF THE DAY

Love your neighbor as yourself

(MATTHEW 22:39B)

BLESSINGS THE DAY BROUGHT ME

_____
_____
_____
_____
_____
_____

DOODLE OF THE DAY!

M T W TH F S SU   DATE: ___ / ___ / ___

I THANK THE LORD FOR

1. _____
2. _____
3. _____

TODAY I WILL STRIVE TO BE:

_____

BIBLE VERSE OF THE DAY | *And remember, I am with you always, to the end of the age*

(MATTHEW 28:20B)

BLESSINGS THE DAY BROUGHT ME

_____
_____
_____
_____

DOODLE OF THE DAY!

| M | T | W | TH | F | S | SU | DATE: ___ / ___ / ___ |

I THANK THE LORD FOR

1. _____
2. _____
3. _____

TODAY I WILL STRIVE TO BE:

_____

BIBLE VERSE OF THE DAY

Holy, holy, holy, is the Lord

(ISAIAH 6:3B)

BLESSINGS THE DAY BROUGHT ME

_____
_____
_____
_____
_____

DOODLE OF THE DAY!

M T W TH F S SU   DATE: __/__/__

I THANK THE LORD FOR

1. _____
2. _____
3. _____

TODAY I WILL STRIVE TO BE:

_____

BIBLE VERSE OF THE DAY | *Seek good and not evil*

(AMOS 5:14A)

BLESSINGS THE DAY BROUGHT ME

_____
_____
_____
_____
_____

DOODLE OF THE DAY!

M T W TH F S SU   DATE: ___/___/___

I THANK THE LORD FOR

1. _____
2. _____
3. _____

TODAY I WILL STRIVE TO BE:

_____

BIBLE VERSE OF THE DAY | *My lips will not speak unjustly, and my tongue will not utter deceit*

(JOB 27:4)

BLESSINGS THE DAY BROUGHT ME

_____
_____
_____
_____
_____

DOODLE OF THE DAY!

M T W TH F S SU   DATE: ___/___/___

I THANK THE LORD FOR

1. _____
2. _____
3. _____

TODAY I WILL STRIVE TO BE:

_____

BIBLE VERSE OF THE DAY

When I am afraid, I will trust in You

(PSALM 56:3)

BLESSINGS THE DAY BROUGHT ME

_____
_____
_____
_____
_____

DOODLE OF THE DAY!

M T W TH F S SU   DATE: ___ / ___ / ___

I THANK THE LORD FOR

1. _____
2. _____
3. _____

TODAY I WILL STRIVE TO BE:

_____

BIBLE VERSE OF THE DAY

God's faithful love endures forever

(PSALM 107:1B)

BLESSINGS THE DAY BROUGHT ME

_____
_____
_____
_____
_____

DOODLE OF THE DAY!

M T W TH F S SU   DATE: ___ / ___ / ___

I THANK THE LORD FOR

1. _____
2. _____
3. _____

TODAY I WILL STRIVE TO BE:

_____

BIBLE VERSE OF THE DAY | *I have treasured Your word in my heart so that I may not sin against You*

(PSALM 119:11)

BLESSINGS THE DAY BROUGHT ME

_____
_____
_____
_____
_____

DOODLE OF THE DAY!

M   T   W   TH   F   S   SU   DATE: ___ / ___ / ___

I THANK THE LORD FOR

1. _____
2. _____
3. _____

TODAY I WILL STRIVE TO BE:

_____

BIBLE VERSE OF THE DAY | *Trust in the Lord with all your heart, do not rely on your own understanding*

(PROVERBS 3:5)

BLESSINGS THE DAY BROUGHT ME

_____
_____
_____
_____
_____

DOODLE OF THE DAY!

M T W TH F S SU DATE: ___/___/___

I THANK THE LORD FOR

1. _____
2. _____
3. _____

TODAY I WILL STRIVE TO BE:

_____

BIBLE VERSE OF THE DAY

Guard your heart above all else, for it is the source of life

(PROVERBS 4:23)

BLESSINGS THE DAY BROUGHT ME

_____
_____
_____
_____
_____

DOODLE OF THE DAY!

M T W TH F S SU   DATE: ___ / ___ / ___

I THANK THE LORD FOR

1. _____
2. _____
3. _____

TODAY I WILL STRIVE TO BE:

_____

BIBLE VERSE OF THE DAY | *Keep my commands and live; protect my teachings as the pupil of your eye*

(PROVERBS 7:2)

BLESSINGS THE DAY BROUGHT ME

_____

_____

_____

_____

_____

DOODLE OF THE DAY!

M T W TH F S SU   DATE: __ / __ / __

I THANK THE LORD FOR

1. _____
2. _____
3. _____

TODAY I WILL STRIVE TO BE:

_____

BIBLE VERSE OF THE DAY

There is an occasion for everything, and a time for every activity under heaven

(ECCLESIASTES 3:1)

BLESSINGS THE DAY BROUGHT ME

_____
_____
_____
_____
_____

DOODLE OF THE DAY!

| M | T | W | TH | F | S | SU | DATE: ___/___/___ |

I THANK THE LORD FOR

1. _____
2. _____
3. _____

TODAY I WILL STRIVE TO BE:

_____

BIBLE VERSE OF THE DAY | *The Lord God will help me*

(ISAIAH 50:7A)

BLESSINGS THE DAY BROUGHT ME

_____
_____
_____
_____
_____

DOODLE OF THE DAY!

M T W TH F S SU DATE: ___/___/___

I THANK THE LORD FOR

1. _____
2. _____
3. _____

TODAY I WILL STRIVE TO BE:

_____

BIBLE VERSE OF THE DAY

You cannot be slaves of God and of money

(MATTHEW 6:24C)

BLESSINGS THE DAY BROUGHT ME

_____
_____
_____
_____
_____

DOODLE OF THE DAY!

M T W TH F S SU   DATE: ___/___/___

I THANK THE LORD FOR

1. _____
2. _____
3. _____

TODAY I WILL STRIVE TO BE:

_____

BIBLE VERSE OF THE DAY | *Every good tree produces good fruit, but a bad tree produces bad fruit*

(MATTHEW 7:17)

BLESSINGS THE DAY BROUGHT ME

_____
_____
_____
_____
_____

DOODLE OF THE DAY!

M   T   W   TH   F   S   SU   DATE: ___ / ___ / ___

I THANK THE LORD FOR

1. _____
2. _____
3. _____

TODAY I WILL STRIVE TO BE:

_____

BIBLE VERSE OF THE DAY

Life was in Him, and that life was the light of men

(JOHN 1:4)

BLESSINGS THE DAY BROUGHT ME

_____
_____
_____
_____
_____

DOODLE OF THE DAY!

M T W TH F S SU   DATE: ___ / ___ / ___

I THANK THE LORD FOR

1. _____
2. _____
3. _____

TODAY I WILL STRIVE TO BE:

_____

BIBLE VERSE OF THE DAY | *Be diligent to present yourself approved to God*

(2 TIMOTHY 2:15A)

BLESSINGS THE DAY BROUGHT ME

_____
_____
_____
_____
_____

DOODLE OF THE DAY!

M T W TH F S SU   DATE: ___/___/___

I THANK THE LORD FOR

1. _____

2. _____

3. _____

TODAY I WILL STRIVE TO BE:

_____

BIBLE VERSE OF THE DAY | *Give thanks in everything, for this is God's will for you in Christ Jesus*

(1 THESSALONIANS 5:18)

BLESSINGS THE DAY BROUGHT ME

_____

_____

_____

_____

_____

DOODLE OF THE DAY!

M T W TH F S SU   DATE: __ / __ / __

I THANK THE LORD FOR

1. _____
2. _____
3. _____

TODAY I WILL STRIVE TO BE:

_____

BIBLE VERSE OF THE DAY | *Man's anger does not accomplish God's righteousness*

(JAMES 1:20)

BLESSINGS THE DAY BROUGHT ME

_____
_____
_____
_____
_____

DOODLE OF THE DAY!

M T W TH F S SU   DATE: ___ / ___ / ___

I THANK THE LORD FOR

1. _____
2. _____
3. _____

TODAY I WILL STRIVE TO BE:

_____

BIBLE VERSE OF THE DAY | *For this is what love for God is: to keep His commands*

(1 JOHN 5:3A)

BLESSINGS THE DAY BROUGHT ME

_____
_____
_____
_____
_____

DOODLE OF THE DAY!

M T W TH F S SU DATE: ___ / ___ / ___

I THANK THE LORD FOR

1. _____
2. _____
3. _____

TODAY I WILL STRIVE TO BE:

_____

BIBLE VERSE OF THE DAY | *We love because He first loved us*

(1 JOHN 4:19)

BLESSINGS THE DAY BROUGHT ME

_____
_____
_____
_____
_____

DOODLE OF THE DAY!

M T W TH F S SU   DATE: ___ / ___ / ___

I THANK THE LORD FOR

1. _____
2. _____
3. _____

TODAY I WILL STRIVE TO BE:

_____

BIBLE VERSE OF THE DAY | *I know that the Lord is great*

(PSALM 135:5A)

BLESSINGS THE DAY BROUGHT ME

_____
_____
_____
_____
_____

DOODLE OF THE DAY!

M T W TH F S SU   DATE: __/__/__

I THANK THE LORD FOR

1. _____
2. _____
3. _____

TODAY I WILL STRIVE TO BE:

_____

BIBLE VERSE OF THE DAY	*I will give You thanks with all my heart*

(PSALM 138:1)

BLESSINGS THE DAY BROUGHT ME

_____
_____
_____
_____
_____

DOODLE OF THE DAY!

M T W TH F S SU   DATE: __ / __ / __

I THANK THE LORD FOR

1. _____
2. _____
3. _____

TODAY I WILL STRIVE TO BE:

_____

BIBLE VERSE OF THE DAY | *Think about Him in all your ways, and He will guide you on the right paths*

(PROV 3:6)

BLESSINGS THE DAY BROUGHT ME

_____
_____
_____
_____
_____

DOODLE OF THE DAY!

M T W TH F S SU   DATE: ___ / ___ / ___

I THANK THE LORD FOR

1. _____
2. _____
3. _____

TODAY I WILL STRIVE TO BE:

_____

BIBLE VERSE OF THE DAY | *The Lord is good to everyone*

(PSALM 145:9A)

BLESSINGS THE DAY BROUGHT ME

_____
_____
_____
_____
_____

DOODLE OF THE DAY!

M T W TH F S SU   DATE: ___/___/___

I THANK THE LORD FOR

1. _____
2. _____
3. _____

TODAY I WILL STRIVE TO BE:

_____

BIBLE VERSE OF THE DAY | *An honest witness does not deceive, but a dishonest witness utters lies*

(PROVERBS 14:5)

BLESSINGS THE DAY BROUGHT ME

_____
_____
_____
_____
_____
_____

DOODLE OF THE DAY!

M T W TH F S SU   DATE: ___/___/___

I THANK THE LORD FOR

1. _____

2. _____

3. _____

TODAY I WILL STRIVE TO BE:

_____

BIBLE VERSE OF THE DAY | *Don't let your spirit rush to be angry, for anger abides in the heart of fools*

(ECCLESIASTES 7:9)

BLESSINGS THE DAY BROUGHT ME

_____

_____

_____

_____

_____

DOODLE OF THE DAY!

M   T   W   TH   F   S   SU   DATE: ___ / ___ / ___

I THANK THE LORD FOR

1. _____
2. _____
3. _____

TODAY I WILL STRIVE TO BE:

_____

BIBLE VERSE OF THE DAY | *All scripture is inspired by God*

(2 TIMOTHY 3:16A)

BLESSINGS THE DAY BROUGHT ME

_____
_____
_____
_____
_____

DOODLE OF THE DAY!

M T W TH F S SU   DATE: __/__/__

I THANK THE LORD FOR

1. _____
2. _____
3. _____

TODAY I WILL STRIVE TO BE:

_____

BIBLE VERSE OF THE DAY | *My sheep hear My voice, I know them, and they follow Me*

(JOHN 10:27)

BLESSINGS THE DAY BROUGHT ME

_____
_____
_____
_____
_____

DOODLE OF THE DAY!

M T W TH F S SU   DATE: ___ /___ /___

I THANK THE LORD FOR

1. _____
2. _____
3. _____

TODAY I WILL STRIVE TO BE:

_____

BIBLE VERSE OF THE DAY | *Rejoice with those who rejoice; weep with those who weep*

(ROMANS 12:15)

BLESSINGS THE DAY BROUGHT ME

_____
_____
_____
_____
_____

DOODLE OF THE DAY!

M T W TH F S SU   DATE: ___ / ___ / ___

I THANK THE LORD FOR

1. _____
2. _____
3. _____

TODAY I WILL STRIVE TO BE:

_____

BIBLE VERSE OF THE DAY | *Don't grieve God's Holy Spirit. You were sealed by Him for the day of redemption*

(EPHESIANS 4:30)

BLESSINGS THE DAY BROUGHT ME

_____
_____
_____
_____

DOODLE OF THE DAY!

M   T   W   TH   F   S   SU   DATE: ___/___/___

I THANK THE LORD FOR

1. _____
2. _____
3. _____

TODAY I WILL STRIVE TO BE:

_____

BIBLE VERSE OF THE DAY | *Keep yourselves in the love of God, expecting the mercy of our Lord Jesus Christ*

(JUDE 1:21)

BLESSINGS THE DAY BROUGHT ME

_____
_____
_____
_____
_____

DOODLE OF THE DAY!

M T W TH F S SU   DATE: ___/___/___

I THANK THE LORD FOR

1. _____
2. _____
3. _____

TODAY I WILL STRIVE TO BE:

_____

BIBLE VERSE OF THE DAY | *Children, obey your parents as you would the Lord, because this is right*

(EPHESIANS 6:1)

BLESSINGS THE DAY BROUGHT ME

_____
_____
_____
_____
_____

DOODLE OF THE DAY!

M T W TH F S SU   DATE: ___/___/___

I THANK THE LORD FOR

1. _____
2. _____
3. _____

TODAY I WILL STRIVE TO BE:

_____

BIBLE VERSE OF THE DAY

Whatever you do, in word or in deed, do everything in the name of the Lord Jesus

(COLOSSIANS 3:17)

BLESSINGS THE DAY BROUGHT ME

_____
_____
_____
_____
_____

DOODLE OF THE DAY!

M   T   W   TH   F   S   SU   DATE: ___ / ___ / ___

I THANK THE LORD FOR

1. _____
2. _____
3. _____

TODAY I WILL STRIVE TO BE:

_____

BIBLE VERSE OF THE DAY | *Your word is a lamp for my feet and a light on my path*

(PSALM 119:105)

BLESSINGS THE DAY BROUGHT ME

_____
_____
_____
_____

DOODLE OF THE DAY!

M T W TH F S SU   DATE: ___/___/___

I THANK THE LORD FOR

1. _____
2. _____
3. _____

TODAY I WILL STRIVE TO BE:

_____

BIBLE VERSE OF THE DAY

Let everything that breathes praise the Lord. Hallelujah!

(PSALM 150:6)

BLESSINGS THE DAY BROUGHT ME

_____
_____
_____
_____
_____

DOODLE OF THE DAY!

M T W TH F S SU   DATE: ___ / ___ / ___

I THANK THE LORD FOR

1. _____
2. _____
3. _____

TODAY I WILL STRIVE TO BE:

_____

BIBLE VERSE OF THE DAY | *Righteousness exalts a nation, but sin is a disgrace to any people*

(PROVERBS 14:34)

BLESSINGS THE DAY BROUGHT ME

_____
_____
_____
_____
_____

DOODLE OF THE DAY!

M T W TH F S SU   DATE: ___/___/___

I THANK THE LORD FOR

1. _____
2. _____
3. _____

TODAY I WILL STRIVE TO BE:

_____

BIBLE VERSE OF THE DAY | *Do not fear for I am with you*

(ISAIAH 43:5A)

BLESSINGS THE DAY BROUGHT ME

_____
_____
_____
_____
_____

DOODLE OF THE DAY!

M T W TH F S SU   DATE: ___ / ___ / ___

I THANK THE LORD FOR

1. _____
2. _____
3. _____

TODAY I WILL STRIVE TO BE:

_____

BIBLE VERSE OF THE DAY | *The man who trusts in the Lord, whose confidence indeed is the Lord, is blessed*

(JEREMIAH 17:7)

BLESSINGS THE DAY BROUGHT ME

_____
_____
_____
_____
_____

DOODLE OF THE DAY!

M T W TH F S SU   DATE: ___ / ___ / ___

I THANK THE LORD FOR

1. _____
2. _____
3. _____

TODAY I WILL STRIVE TO BE:

_____

BIBLE VERSE OF THE DAY | *Shout joyfully to God, all the earth!*

(PSALM 66:1)

BLESSINGS THE DAY BROUGHT ME

_____
_____
_____
_____
_____

DOODLE OF THE DAY!

M T W TH F S SU DATE: ___/___/___

I THANK THE LORD FOR

1. _____
2. _____
3. _____

TODAY I WILL STRIVE TO BE:

_____

BIBLE VERSE OF THE DAY | *As a deer longs for streams of water, so I long for You, God*

(PSALM 42:1)

BLESSINGS THE DAY BROUGHT ME

_____
_____
_____
_____
_____

DOODLE OF THE DAY!

M T W TH F S SU   DATE: ___/___/___

I THANK THE LORD FOR

1. _____
2. _____
3. _____

TODAY I WILL STRIVE TO BE:

_____

BIBLE VERSE OF THE DAY

Make Your ways known to me, Lord; teach me Your paths

(PSALM 25:4)

BLESSINGS THE DAY BROUGHT ME

_____
_____
_____
_____
_____
_____

DOODLE OF THE DAY!

M T W TH F S SU   DATE: __/__/__

I THANK THE LORD FOR

1. _____
2. _____
3. _____

TODAY I WILL STRIVE TO BE:

_____

BIBLE VERSE OF THE DAY | *I lie down and sleep; I wake again because the Lord sustains me*

(PSALM 3:5)

BLESSINGS THE DAY BROUGHT ME

_____
_____
_____
_____
_____

DOODLE OF THE DAY!

M T W TH F S SU   DATE: __ / __ / __

I THANK THE LORD FOR

1. _____
2. _____
3. _____

TODAY I WILL STRIVE TO BE:

_____

BIBLE VERSE OF THE DAY

The Lord is my Shepherd; there is nothing I lack

(PSALM 23:1)

BLESSINGS THE DAY BROUGHT ME

_____
_____
_____
_____
_____

DOODLE OF THE DAY!

M T W TH F S SU   DATE: ___/___/___

I THANK THE LORD FOR

1. _____
2. _____
3. _____

TODAY I WILL STRIVE TO BE:

_____

BIBLE VERSE OF THE DAY | *Stop your fighting and know that I am God, exalted among the nations*

(PSALM 46:10)

BLESSINGS THE DAY BROUGHT ME

_____
_____
_____
_____
_____

DOODLE OF THE DAY!

M T W TH F S SU DATE: ___/___/___

I THANK THE LORD FOR

1. _____
2. _____
3. _____

TODAY I WILL STRIVE TO BE:

_____

BIBLE VERSE OF THE DAY | *Give thanks to Him and praise His name*

(PSALM 100:4)

BLESSINGS THE DAY BROUGHT ME

_____
_____
_____
_____

DOODLE OF THE DAY!

M T W TH F S SU DATE: ___ / ___ / ___

I THANK THE LORD FOR

1. _____
2. _____
3. _____

TODAY I WILL STRIVE TO BE:

_____

BIBLE VERSE OF THE DAY | *Even the winds and sea obey him*

(MATTHEW 8:27B)

BLESSINGS THE DAY BROUGHT ME

_____
_____
_____
_____
_____

DOODLE OF THE DAY!

M T W TH F S SU   DATE: ___/___/___

I THANK THE LORD FOR

1. _____
2. _____
3. _____

TODAY I WILL STRIVE TO BE:

_____

BIBLE VERSE OF THE DAY | *Do not have other gods besides Me*

(EXODUS 20:3)

BLESSINGS THE DAY BROUGHT ME

_____
_____
_____
_____
_____

DOODLE OF THE DAY!

M T W TH F S SU   DATE: ___ / ___ / ___

I THANK THE LORD FOR

1. _____
2. _____
3. _____

TODAY I WILL STRIVE TO BE:

_____

BIBLE VERSE OF THE DAY | *The day is Yours, also the night; You established the moon and the sun*

(PSALM 74:16)

BLESSINGS THE DAY BROUGHT ME

_____
_____
_____
_____
_____

DOODLE OF THE DAY!

M   T   W   TH   F   S   SU   DATE: ___ / ___ / ___

I THANK THE LORD FOR

1. _____
2. _____
3. _____

TODAY I WILL STRIVE TO BE:

_____

BIBLE VERSE OF THE DAY | *Is anything too hard for the Lord?*

(GENESIS 18:14A)

BLESSINGS THE DAY BROUGHT ME

_____
_____
_____
_____
_____

DOODLE OF THE DAY!

M   T   W   TH   F   S   SU   DATE: ___ / ___ / ___

I THANK THE LORD FOR

1. _____
2. _____
3. _____

TODAY I WILL STRIVE TO BE:

_____

BIBLE VERSE OF THE DAY | *Do not misuse the name of the Lord*

(EXODUS 20:7A)

BLESSINGS THE DAY BROUGHT ME

_____
_____
_____
_____

DOODLE OF THE DAY!

M T W TH F S SU DATE: ___ / ___ / ___

I THANK THE LORD FOR

1. _____
2. _____
3. _____

TODAY I WILL STRIVE TO BE:

_____

BIBLE VERSE OF THE DAY | *Now therefore, our God, we give You thanks and praise Your glorious name*

(I CHRONICLES 29:13)

BLESSINGS THE DAY BROUGHT ME

_____
_____
_____
_____
_____

DOODLE OF THE DAY!

M   T   W   TH   F   S   SU   DATE: ___ / ___ / ___

I THANK THE LORD FOR

1. _____
2. _____
3. _____

TODAY I WILL STRIVE TO BE:

_____

BIBLE VERSE OF THE DAY | *The heavens declare the glory of God*

(PSALM 19:1)

BLESSINGS THE DAY BROUGHT ME

_____
_____
_____
_____
_____

DOODLE OF THE DAY!

M   T   W   TH   F   S   SU   DATE: ___ / ___ / ___

I THANK THE LORD FOR

1. _____
2. _____
3. _____

TODAY I WILL STRIVE TO BE:

_____

BIBLE VERSE OF THE DAY | *Therefore, if anyone is in Christ, he is a new creation*

(2 CORINTHIANS 5:17)

BLESSINGS THE DAY BROUGHT ME

_____
_____
_____
_____
_____

DOODLE OF THE DAY!

M T W TH F S SU   DATE: ___ / ___ / ___

I THANK THE LORD FOR

1. _____
2. _____
3. _____

TODAY I WILL STRIVE TO BE:

_____

BIBLE VERSE OF THE DAY | *The Lord your God is with you*

(JOSHUA 1:9)

BLESSINGS THE DAY BROUGHT ME

_____
_____
_____
_____
_____

DOODLE OF THE DAY!

Made in United States
North Haven, CT
19 September 2022

24303101R00057